Navigating Change

THE HALIʻA ALOHA SERIES

Navigating Change

VALDEANE UCHIMA ODACHI

THE HALIʻA ALOHA SERIES

Darien Hsu Gee, Series Editor

Haliʻa Aloha ("cherished memories") by Legacy Isle Publishing is a guided memoir program developed in collaboration with series editor Darien Hsu Gee. The series celebrates moments big and small, harnessing the power of short forms to preserve the lived experiences of the storytellers. To become a Haliʻa Aloha author, please visit www.legacyislepublishing.net.

Legacy Isle Publishing is an imprint of Watermark Publishing, based in Honolulu, Hawaiʻi, and dedicated to "Telling Hawaiʻi's Stories" through memoirs, corporate biographies, family histories and other books.

Most of the names in this book have been changed to protect the privacy of the individuals involved.

All photos courtesy of the author.

ISBN 978-1-948011-75-4 (print)
ISBN 978-1-948011-76-1 (ebook)

Design and production
Dawn Sakamoto Paiva

Legacy Isle Publishing
1000 Bishop St., Ste. 806
Honolulu, HI 96813
Telephone 1-808-587-7766
Toll-free 1-866-900-BOOK
www.legacyislepublishing.net

Printed in the United States

For Nai'a and Nolan

CONTENTS

I.

WHAT'S IN A NAME?

My birth name, Valdeane Akeko Uchima held little appeal to me as a child.

Valdeane. My first name is that of my mother's coworker from the National Educational Association (NEA) in Washington, DC. My mom fell in love with the name and received permission to use it if she had a daughter. My first name was difficult to spell, even for family members. Teachers who read my name for the first (or even second and third) time had a difficult time pronouncing it. "Val-dah-nay? Val-dee-ann? Val-dee-annie? Valerie?" Nope. My mom didn't know the meaning of the name nor the ethnic origins, and though it didn't bother her, it left me feeling empty and lacking in personal identity.

Akeko. My middle name came from my father mishearing the common Japanese name, Akiko, gifted by his maternal grandmother. It was pointed out repeatedly when I attended Japanese school during my elementary years. Despite my continued insistence, the Japanese language teachers would constantly "correct" me, insisting that my name was in fact pronounced "Ah-kee-koh" and *not* "Ah-keh-koh."

Uchima. My last name was uncommon in my hometown. With no older siblings or cousins with the same last name, I longed to be like other classmates who benefited from the positive effects of teachers knowing their family members.

The names that caused me so much discomfort as a child are now my unique marker. Marrying my spouse, with his unique family name of Odachi, further added to the distinctive nature of my identity. Being unique is no longer something I am ashamed of. But after forty-eight years of life, I'd really appreciate it if all my relatives could spell my name correctly!

EXHILARATION ON THE OCEAN

Splash! Cold sea spray drenches me between my mother's attempts to clear my view with a sweep of her hand. The seawater drips down my hair and face, the sharp, salty droplets delighting my tastebuds. Water seeps beneath my blue bathing suit and the bright orange life jacket my mother put on me at my father's urging.

A dull buzz radiates through my tiny fingers, numb from tightly gripping the slick, wet frame of the boat's windshield. As our small vessel breaks through the foamy white face of each oncoming surge, it causes the boat to land with a hard *thump* as we fall off the backside of each wave, causing me to shriek in excitement. Elation swells through my entire being as I voyage on Mother Nature's liquid roller coaster ride.

This day on the ocean is one of the strongest and most joyous memories I have of being in my dad's boat. My father and I view that day quite differently. He recently mentioned the sudden change of weather and the developing rough seas took him by surprise.

He was concerned for our safety and though he was an experienced waterman, it remains one of the only times he was truly scared while out on the ocean.

For me, that was my best day out on the ocean. I was held securely around the waist by my mother, with my father piloting the boat back toward the harbor. I was safe. I was treasured. I was loved.

SMALL KID TIME HIGHS AND LOWS

It's my seventh birthday and we are at a small pizza parlor, just across the street from Big Way Market in my hometown. My birthday is two days before Halloween and by that time, my mom has usually finished my Halloween costume, so the celebration is often a costume party. This was one area of my young life that my parents excelled at. My mom lovingly sewed my attire, and with the help of my dad's woodworking skills, I often had the best homemade Halloween costume, better than most my peers.

For this birthday celebration, I am dressed as Jana of the Jungle, a character from a Saturday morning cartoon. Adorned in a short, leopard print dress, I'm feeling sassy in my handmade outfit. Jana is a female hero who was lost in the jungle as a child and raised by the indigenous people of the area. She wears a necklace that can be used as a throwing weapon, and her best friend is a white jaguar.

A family friend two years younger than me arrives dressed as Wonder Woman. I smugly notice that her costume is store-bought, not handmade like *my* Wonder Woman costume from a couple years before, which was carefully sewn by my mother. She had embellished it with a hand-cut emblem, carefully appliqued onto a red halter top. White stars studded a pair of blue shorts, and the golden tiara, magic lasso, bracelets and high stockings completed the look. Not a perfect replica of Lynda Carter's Wonder Woman costume, but definitely *not* store-bought.

My proud reflection is overshadowed by the oversized balloon the pizza parlor owners gifted me. It is about four feet long and twelve inches in diameter, taller than me, and the largest balloon I've ever seen. I barely get to play with it before my older cousin B takes it outside to play with his friend. They toss it back and forth to each other. I wince when it drops onto the hot asphalt with a sudden, deflating *pop*. "My balloon!"

Thankfully, I am distracted from this disappointing moment, as it's time to open gifts. A friend brought a present that has captured my attention since he arrived. There is an adorable stuffed animal secured to the top of the gift with a bow. I can't figure out if it's a bear or dog, especially since it's adorned with what resembles a blue and white striped suit and has a bow tie made of soft red felt. I surrender the need to know as I struggle to untangle the tight plastic ribbon it's secured with. I name him Henry, and he becomes my favorite stuffed friend.

LOST TIME

It's the Thanksgiving after my eighth birthday and the noise of the family party fills our home. My teenage cousin Jiro has taken a sudden interest in me and my assortment of stuffed animals. In a seemingly Herculean effort, he carries all of them, including a stuffed bear that's almost four feet tall, from my bedroom. He pauses at the edge of the living room, amusing the family with his skill and grip strength, and provides me with a slight swelling of pride as my collection of animals garnish oohs and aahs from the family. I accompany him back to my bedroom and tuck each animal under the blankets of my bed as if settling them in for a nap.

Jiro and I sit on my bed among the stuffed animals, covers pulled up over us as we watch the football game. I'm startled when his probing hands find their way beneath the fabric of my mint green terrycloth shorts. I'm frozen, as still as possible.

Jiro's brother appears at the doorway and casually asks, "What's happening?"

"Just watching the game," Jiro says nonchalantly.

It feels like an eternity when, without any urging, my dear Henry rolls off the bed, his stuffed self just out of reach. It seems like forever before I roll my body off the bed while exclaiming, "I need to grab Henry!" I lock myself in my parents' bedroom, claiming I have homework, until everyone departs.

THE RED SWEATER

During my tween years, it was a toss-up if I should wear a bra to school. This would soon change from "if" to "must" when I learned how cruel schoolmates could be.

My favorite piece of clothing was a long sleeve, zip up sweater. With velvety red fabric, it was like a portable security blanket. The ribbed collar and cuffs hugged my neck and wrists, not too loose nor too tight. Unlike the Chic jeans and noisy Clark Chang slippers a lot of girls wore, no one else had a sweater like mine. It was luxurious and unique.

The sweater had been gifted to me from my uncle's new wife, a young woman from Korea who seemed graceful and kind. I watched her intently as she made Korean *nori,* broiling the seaweed sheets over the heat of the stove, then brushing them with sesame oil and salt. It was so different from the sweet and shoyu-flavored *ajitsuke* nori that we normally snacked on. She spoke with an exotic accent, and her fitted clothing highlighted her thin frame, different from the pear-shaped bodies of most of my female family members.

As I waited for Japanese school to start after another endless day of public school, I accidentally spilled water down the front of my shirt, which was now soaked. Not wanting to linger in wet clothes, I went to the restroom, and removed my top and zipped up my velvety sweater over my bare chest. Feeling warm and dry, I walked out of the girls' restroom.

One of my classmates approached me. "What's this?" she asked as she gestured toward my sweater. With ninja-like reflexes, she promptly pulled the zipper down the front of my sweater, exposing my naked chest.

Her laughter and the laughter of the other students echoed within the walls of the restroom as I quickly retreated to fix my sweater.

CHILDHOOD TROUBLEMAKER

At the start of my sixth-grade year, in 1984, I have two new friends. I'm excited because I normally have a hard time getting to know people. Most of my schoolmates tease me about my clothes, how my hair is done or that I'm a bad student. I want to impress these new friends and prove I'm cool.

When my grandparents are away from home to help my uncle on the family farm, I take my new friends to my grandparents' house. I break in by loosening the removable screen from a lower window of the house. I crawl through the open space and let the girls in via the back door. While inside, I take a bunch of coins hidden in the master bedroom closet that belonged to my uncle. As I depart, I pluck the blossoms of my grandmother's treasured purple orchid, stomping on it with my pink glitter jelly sandal in a misguided attempt to prove to the girls that I'm tough.

The next day, bursting with guilt, I deposit some of the stolen coins on top of various books in the school library, hoping to distribute my shame along with the evidence. However, I am an unskilled thief and unsuccessfully try to hide a stash of coins in my messy classroom desk. Classmates soon inform the teacher that I'm storing a small fortune among my belongings.

My parents are called, and I'm forced to reveal the stolen goods. I'm certain that everyone in school knows I have done something horribly wrong. After school, my mom drives me to the homes of different relatives to repeatedly admit my sin, be scolded and looked at with shaming eyes that dart aside as if the seer is tainted by my evil act.

IMAGERY INTERRUPTED

When Mom picks me up from school for an orthodontist appointment one afternoon, my teacher seizes the opportunity to discuss my poor grades and insubordinate behavior. Mom's anger fills the car with silence during our ride out of town. The return journey is no better, and I try to hide by sinking into the passenger seat of our brown Toyota station wagon.

Mom glances left to check her blind spot and begins to merge into the fast-moving traffic onto the H-2 freeway headed west. Out of the corner of her eye, she sees a large white truck move into her lane. To avoid a collision, she swerves, initiating an uncontrollable game of tug-o-war with the steering wheel. She loses control of the car, and we are suddenly upside down. Imagining that we are teetering on the edge of the overpass, I scream, telling Mom not to move.

Interrupting my frightening mental image, a pair of hands appear above me. Strong arms swiftly lift me out of the passenger side window of our Toyota station wagon, and I emerge, realizing the car has turned over onto the driver's side. I am placed on the ground as my mom is pulled from the car. People surround her, wrapping her bloody arm out of sight. The rush of activity around us is dizzying. We are moved to the side of the freeway as the afternoon traffic buzzes by in neighboring lanes.

Accustomed to being the cause of the strife in my family, I blame myself. *This accident is my fault. I'm a horrible person. Mom and Dad would be happier without me.* Standing aside from the commotion surrounding my mom, I turn around to grasp the concrete wall of the freeway, peering over the edge to the road below. I can swing my leg over the concrete siding and slip over the edge without anyone noticing. As the thought urges my body forward, a hand grasps my shoulder and a voice instructs me to sit. I feel the warm concrete beneath me, the afternoon heat numbing me of my guilt before I am ushered into an ambulance with my mom.

CAMPING TRIP

A favorite family pastime was camping with my dad's fishing buddies and their families. On occasion, my father's other daughter, my older half sister Lauryl, would join us to my delight.

In the evenings, we'd engage in a type of scavenger hunt to gather what we thought were gigantic *pipipi,* small edible mollusks that gather on the rocky shorelines. We'd boil them atop a propane camp stove and pluck out the chewy innards with an open safety pin. They were slightly salty and had the texture of a clam. More of an activity than a meal, it was one of my favorite things to do while camping. Only later I learned that the shells we gathered were actually *kūpeʻe,* an edible marine snail, valued for their large shells of varying patterns, used decoratively and as adornments in the practice of hula. Too bad we didn't keep those precious shells!

One night, Lauryl and Dad went walking along the beach. When they returned, Lauryl was clutching a large ghost crab in each hand. The giant crabs came out at night and could be easily captured while out of their burrows. I admired my sister's bravery but recoiled at the thought of restraining the sandy behemoths with their pinching claws and scratchy arachnid-like bodies.

The following day, in an attempt to delay our departure as we broke down camp, Lauryl amused herself by jumping on the tarp Dad was folding. Always wanting to emulate her, I followed suit. Dad reached out, grabbed Lauryl's hand and quickly moved her off the tarp. But when Dad grabbed my arm to move me, a loud unnatural pop was heard. My arm flopped down, dislocated at the shoulder. I was rushed to the nearest hospital, my arm reset and placed in a sling. To this day, Dad claims I must have faked the injury since I reached up with my injured arm to effortlessly open the back door when we arrived home.

GRANDPARENTAL BABYSITTING SERVICE

Grandma and Grandpa had retired from farming and moved into the home they had built in my hometown. My parents and I lived up the street, far enough to be separated from my grandparents, but close enough to visit daily, their house becoming my refuge for company and snacks.

Being the only child, I had no siblings to rely on or be responsible for after school. My father's other daughter lived with her mother in Moanalua Valley, and I only saw her on the weekends, so Grandpa and Grandma were my before and after school companions.

On school days, I was dropped off early in the morning, often before dawn as my parents headed to work. Grandma made sure I woke up and got to school on time. I couldn't count on them for a ride since Grandma didn't drive and Grandpa refused to drive me. After all, if he could cross five rivers to get to school in his day, I could definitely walk the quarter mile to school. Though the walk wasn't far, I envied the other children who were dropped off and picked up daily.

After school, I would head to my grandparents' house where I could expect afternoon soap operas and Grandpa's four o'clock cocktail hour with appetizers of American cheese, divided in four and sized just right to sit atop a Diamond Bakery soda cracker. These snacks accompanied Grandpa's glass of Jim Beam whiskey, thinned with water poured from a pink plastic hospital pitcher. I would sit and talk story with my grandparents, chatting away while Grandpa scowled at me, a reminder that I was too talkative for him.

Cocktail hour transitioned to dinner as Grandma brought out small dishes of prepared food for Grandpa to eat. One dish after another, Grandpa would be served a small feast composed of tiny portions of mixed vegetables, pork stir-fried with more vegetables, some tofu or miso soup with thick udon noodles to accompany the meal. Near the end of Grandpa's dining, Grandma would finally sit down to eat the remaining food, eating what Grandpa had left behind.

My day would conclude at five o'clock when my parents picked me up to take me home for the evening.

LOYAL CONFIDANT

Black ball of fur with a white streaked chest,
my four-legged sibling that I loved the best.
No one would listen when I said not to pet him,
they insisted my boy would be fine if I let them.
All of them soon regretted their decision,
after my pup gave each a toothy incision.
Territorial and fierce, his bite was so strong,
luckily, he never held on for too long.
As he got older, his nose would scab and grow,
something was wrong, I told my parents so.
To the vet we took him on one fateful day,
I cried my heart out as I walked away.
Leaving my boy and saying goodbye,
too many tears fell that just couldn't dry.

SIBLINGS, SEATING AND SANDWICHES

I'm riding the city bus with my older half sister. Her directions to me are very clear. If I see someone get on the bus who is older than me or has a hard time standing, and there are no other seats available, I need to get up and offer that person my seat since I am in my tween years, young and strong enough to stand.

Soon after, an older woman gets on the bus and my sister offers the woman her seat. We both rise to give her space and we remain standing. We hold tightly to the upright poles for the duration of our ride, our bodies moving with the forward momentum and periodic braking motion of the bus.

Growing up, I longed to have my sister protect me, counsel me and patiently teach me things. But as we got older, we grew further apart. Her visits became more infrequent as the trajectory of her life took her into adulthood. The memory is a warm reminder of how my sister taught me to be courteous, and I shared the story with my children to perpetuate the same lesson.

In another fond memory, while at the beach, my sister taught me how to make a sandwich of cold cuts, *kimchi* and mayonnaise between two slices of white bread. A salty yet nutritious meal since there were veggies in it and veggies are healthy, right? Absolutely. What a responsible sister!

MULTIPLICATION AND MILKSHAKES

During a particularly difficult fourth-grade year in elementary school, where I simply could not memorize my nine times table, I caught the attention of the principal, Mr. George Nakasone. A calm soul, with a soothing deep voice, Mr. Nakasone was always picking up bits of rubbish as he walked the campus. Students would find his office window open, a welcoming invitation for them to stop by and chat. Engaging in those brief interactions were heartwarming and validating, unlike the stops to the vice principal's office for disciplinary action!

Aware of my mathematical challenges, Mr. Nakasone would take every opportunity to quiz me on my multiplication tables. I'd occasionally spot him first and do my best to escape his impromptu quizzes, but I wasn't able to evade him all the time. He'd catch up to me on the recess field or near the cafeteria after lunch and in the calmest baritone he'd ask, "Valdeane, what's nine times seven?" I usually stammered out the wrong reply, but he kindly and patiently encouraged me to keep studying.

One day, Mr. Nakasone had a proposal. If I was able to memorize the nine times table, he'd reward me with a milkshake from the nearby McDonald's. I'm not sure if it was the tempting incentive or if I finally memorized the table, but Mr. Nakasone was a man of his word, and I found myself, along with another classmate, to be a lucky recipient of a cool, frosty milkshake.

With proof that his offer was fruitful, Mr. Nakasone told me that if I could memorize the entire multiplication table up to the twelves, he'd treat me to another milkshake. I progressed from elementary to intermediate school with the multiplication table memorized, but reluctant to remind Mr. Nakasone of his commitment, I left without securing my final milkshake reward.

Entering my tenth grade history class, I was delighted to learn that my new teacher, Mrs. Nakasone, was the wife of my favorite principal. Her straightforward and upbeat personality encouraged me to actively participate and I was able to achieve better grades in her coursework than in most of my other classes. After that time, I kept in touch with her and her husband. When I graduated from high school, I invited them to my graduation party.

Mr. and Mrs. Nakasone arrived at my party and surprised me by taking out an insulated jug full of strawberry milkshake and three champagne glasses to toast my graduation! Their dedication and my perseverance produced a truly sweet lifelong reward. Not the milkshake nor the strong recall of the nine times table, but a deep love and connection with people who believe in me.

With George Nakasone at the Nakasone residence, Wahiawā, 2020.

SUMMER ON THE NORTH SHORE

In the years following high school, much of my time was spent laying out on the warm beaches of the North Shore of O'ahu with my friend Bernadette, working to perfect my tan. Sitting on the warm sand under the barely-there shade of a coconut tree, we'd chuckle at tourists who became red as ripe lychee fruit while lounging in the sun. Hiding our gaze behind dark glasses, we'd stare at the gorgeous, dark surfer boys headed to the water.

We'd bring *bento,* boxed lunches that contained a crunchy piece of fried chicken, a hearty slice of Spam and sweet strips of teriyaki beef, all on a bed of rice. Chilled cans of orange passionfruit juice filled our cooler. We rarely drank water during those hot days.

Instead of sunscreen, we coated ourselves in layers of tropical scented tanning oil promoted specifically to darken one's skin. We tried our best to shade away our tan lines while staying decent enough not to get thrown off the beach. If we overheated, we ran to the water for a refreshing dunk in the salty waters of the

Pacific, only to emerge and reapply more tanning oil so our skin glistened with incandescent droplets of water.

Before heading home, we'd stop at Matsumoto Shave Ice for vanilla ice cream topped with finely shaved ice. Cool and creamy, they were heavily drizzled with homemade syrups from recipes dating back to the early 1900s, the perfect treat at the end of a hot, sun-soaked day.

Those days would soon give way to the structure of marriage and motherhood. Whenever I catch the scent of coconut oil, I grin as I recall those carefree days on the sun-soaked shores of O'ahu.

II.

A LITTLE BIT ABOUT ME

Impatient child, embattled teen, unfolding adult.
Not seen, not heard, not understood.
Desire and longing give way to grief.
Once alone, now rarely in silence.
Unskilled hands now manage different tasks.
Once distracted and rebellious, now focused.
Thief and liar, policing and teaching.
Challenge and struggle create strong spirit.
Confused and frustrated, now patiently longing.
Searching for meaning, peace and purpose.
Forever talkative yet learning to listen.
Listening for guidance from the ancestors.
Dancing around the joys of life.
Lotsa learning, still growing, not *pau*.

MONEY HIGHS AND WOES

It's 1998. Mike and I are newly married. He teaches second grade at a local elementary school just a few minutes from our small, plantation-style cottage in my hometown of Wahiawā. He is twenty-six years my senior and nearing retirement after twenty plus years of teaching. With Mike's support, I've decided to be unemployed for the first time in a long while, after simultaneously working a full-time position in addition to a part-time job. We live conservatively but finances are tight so I'm excited to learn our first joint tax filing will yield a one-thousand-dollar return. I plan to use this infusion of funds to create a savings account for our unfolding future.

One day, as we are departing our local grocery store, Mike makes a left turn onto the main road and allows our Chevy Monte Carlo to roll between the stalled traffic. He overlooks a slowly approaching sedan, resulting in a fender bender. The other party agrees to avoid the process of filing an insurance claim so they send us two estimates to repair their vehicle. Both quotes are just under a thousand dollars.

My heart sinks. I'm upset that creating a savings account has been delayed by the repair costs of a car accident. It takes me a while to realize that the tax return is exactly enough to cover the expense. I breathe a sigh of relief as I come to understand that the money was available before we needed it!

THE MARATHON

I'm two weeks past my due date. Without requesting permission, my doctor performs an invasive procedure to precipitate labor. A couple days later, after returning home from a leisurely Sunday dinner at my parents' house, my water breaks, a trickle of clear fluid splashing to the floor. We arrive at the hospital after 10:00 p.m., and contractions begin after I start walking around the hospital courtyard. I wrestle the waves of discomfort that intermittently sweep over me.

As night moves into early morning, I am exhausted. The nurse monitoring my progress says my cervix has stopped dilating. I'm stuck at two centimeters—the goal is ten. How is it possible that after five hours of labor, I'm only at two? The baby books state that my cervix will dilate one centimeter each hour.

The books lied.

I strain to get to the bathroom between contractions. I'm barely holding myself together as another wave of pain surges through me. Through tears, I confess to my husband that I don't know how

I'm going to get through another eight hours of labor. I consider getting the epidural I was dead set against.

I am unprepared for this turn of events. What kind of mother will I be if I can't get through the first act of motherhood? I'm embarrassed. I'm depleted. I'm too weak to sustain the natural pain of childbirth. I am a failure.

I'm somewhat calmed by my spouse, my mom and two friends who are there to support me. They remind me that the baby is the goal, and the baby will come no matter what.

Around 4:00 a.m., I make the heartbreaking decision to get the epidural. The hospital staff informs me the anesthesiologist is not on duty until seven o'clock in the morning! I need to labor for three more hours without the relief that I struggled to accept. For the next few hours, I labor through the agony of physical anguish, but also my disappointment to surrender and receive pain-killing drugs.

When the anesthetist and anesthesiologist arrive, I anticipate the calm I know epidurals can provide. But the relief is short-lived, and I request more. After a few more sessions of increased dosages, the male anesthesiologist looks at the squiggly lines on the monitor that represent the contractions and declares that they're manageable. I want to scream, "When was the last time you gave birth to a human, you dumb ass?!" But instead, I swallow my anguish as the next contraction crests, taking the breath out of me.

Though I'm on the maximum dosage, the epidural barely takes the edge off the fierce bite of pain. I strain to stay focused as I breathe through each contraction. At one point I ask my mom to breathe quieter as her heavy breathing is as loud as a leaf blower, distracting my calm. I later learn she was across the room and it was unlikely I could hear her. I am hypersensitive due to the difficulty of labor, and my mom can no longer sit with me as I fight my way through. She calls my dad who picks her up. I realize that I've lost a team member.

At four o'clock in the afternoon, a new anesthetist arrives, thankfully, without the anesthesiologist. He sees that I'm struggling and kindly offers me options. Removal of the epidural in hopes that my body will do what it is supposed to, but will probably be more uncomfortable. Or he could remove the epidural catheter and replace it with a new one. I realize that with the Pitocin flowing, attempting to manage the artificially driven labor will be near impossible, especially since I have been laboring hard since the previous night.

Preparing for the final leg of the marathon, I agree to let him replace the epidural.

The old epidural is removed and when the new one is inserted, I am transported to cloud nine! I finally get to relax with no pain!

Instead of resting, I'm now excited. I chat away as I dilate toward ten centimeters. The nurses tell us that I'm getting close, so Mike applies warm towels to relax my muscles near the birthing site. I suddenly feel a sensation near my bottom and Mike says he can see hair showing in the birth canal. He steps aside and the doctor moves in. I am instructed to push once, twice. I finally cross the finish line of my inaugural birthing event. It's a girl! Our daughter Nai'a is born after twenty-three hours and forty-five minutes of labor. Strong and healthy, she is my well-deserved reward after a day of labor. The next day, Mom and Dad visit their new grandbaby, and it's Mom who smiles the most, holding little Nai'a like a trophy while looking into the camera.

AN UNCERTAIN FUTURE

Mike rocks six-month-old Nai'a while he sits in the master bedroom. I'm standing in the bathroom when I hear Mike play a message from the answering machine. Then the same message is played again. And again, and again. I peek my head into the bedroom and look at Mike as he presses the play button on the answering machine once more.

"What's the matter?" I ask.

He continues to rock Nai'a while he looks at the answering machine quizzically. "I can't remember."

"Can't remember what?"

Mike is great at math but ironically not adept at memorizing phone numbers so I assume he can't recall the phone number left on the message, so I tell him to get a pen and paper to write the message down. He plays the message again.

"Am I still teaching?" he asks.

"Yes," I reply.

His brow is furrowed. "Second grade?"

I think he's joking until I realize he isn't. I call a friend for advice, and after she speaks to Mike over the phone, she advises me to get him to the hospital since he probably experienced a health emergency or was going through one now. She informs me that he could barely remember the day our daughter was born, which was just six months ago.

I place a call to my parents and my dad arrives and takes Mike to Kaiser Hospital in Moanalua. During the drive, Mike keeps asking, "What day is it? What year is it?" My mom arrives soon after to drive the baby and me to join them.

Worst-case scenarios swirl in my mind as we head to the hospital. *I would be a single mother if he died. How would I care for both the baby and Mike if he's disabled?* I appeal to God, the angels and the ancestors. I reach out to Mike's martial arts *sensei,* his teacher who is also a Zen priest and Mike's most respected mentor. He comforts me by saying that all will be well.

The doctor informs us that Mike suffered an event known as transient global amnesia. A nonfatal, temporary condition that self-resolved over the course of a day. The hours when Mike could not recall information was the only time he actually "lost." All other details he had forgotten soon returned. The doctor, like Mike's sensei, assures us that despite the incident, Mike is healthy. And it seems to be so, with nothing more than a couple of hours of lost time.

SWEPT AWAY

I rub my swollen belly and wonder exactly when my second child will decide to enter the world. It's Sunday, March 17, 2002, and Nai'a is just four months shy of her third birthday. The house phone rings. Picking it up, I hear my mom's deliberately calm voice on the other end of the line.

"I don't want you to panic, but Uncle Barney called. He doesn't know where Uncle Victor is."

"What do you mean?" I ask.

"Well, his vehicle is home but the ATV he uses to go to his garden is gone," she says. "Barney went to check Victor's garden, but he didn't see him. He checked the house, and Victor's wallet is still there so he obviously didn't leave the gulch."

"Mom, did Uncle call the police or anything?"

"No. Uncle Barney said he's going to go out at first light tomorrow morning and if he doesn't find Uncle, he'll call the police. Dad is going to go down early to help look." Mike overhears the conversation and volunteers to go.

"Tell Dad to pick Mike up on the way down," I tell her.

Before the sun rises the next morning, Dad and Mike head to the farm to help Uncle Barney search the gulch for any sign of Uncle Victor. Mom, Naiʻa and I soon follow. My two cousins, Vernon and Chad, also join the search.

We arrive in the valley commonly referred to as Kīpapa Gulch, home to my mother's family for three generations. We find a police officer stationed on the concrete parking area of the Arakaki family's former home. The officer informs us that the Honolulu Fire Department's Search and Rescue team have been combing the gulch and will report back to the area.

The police and search crews are amazed at how calm we are. We are hopeful but concerned, knowing that death is no stranger in the valley. From ancient Hawaiian battles to plane crashes and freak accidents, our family understands that many have lost their lives in the vicinity.

The sun moves across the sky, illuminating the valley as morning becomes noon. We wait patiently until we hear the sudden crackle of the police radio, reporting that the search party have found parts of an ATV in the river, lower in the valley. A few minutes later, the radio jumps to life again with the report that a body has been discovered.

The rescue helicopter has been dispatched to retrieve the body. It will land at a nearby park so Uncle Barney and my parents can confirm it's Uncle Victor. My cousins have already headed home so Mike and I take Naiʻa with us to see my grandparents who are waiting at their home in Wahiawā.

We arrive at my grandparents' house and my cousin Chad heads over from next door, where he lives with his brother Vernon, who is still showering after their search. Chad accompanies us to tell Grandma and Grandpa the sad news about Victor.

Grandpa is on his recliner in the living room, watching TV while Grandma sits nearby. I approach him, then kneel, pausing to find the right words. Grandpa looks up at me and sees Chad alongside.

"Grandpa, you know Victor was missing, yeah? Dad, Mike, Vernon and Chad went to the gulch to look for him. The police and fire department too."

"Yeah." Grandpa acknowledges with a short word and nod of his head.

With sadness in my voice, I say, "Grandpa, Victor died."

Grandpa looks from me to Chad, and in the surrounding empty space near us, his expression turns to shock.

"What?! Vernon died too?!"

"No, Grandpa, Victor! *Victor* died!"

I look at Chad. Both of us can barely contain our laughter in this otherwise somber moment.

"Oh, Victor!" Grandpa says.

"Yes, Grandpa. They found him in the river," I confirm.

"Oh, yeah, I knew he was missing but I thought you said Vernon died too!"

We all chuckle at the misunderstanding, a momentary release in a time of sorrow.

SUSPICION

Grandma tells me about her missing jewelry, her eyes darting from me, down to the ground and back again. I suggest that her house cleaner could have moved or stolen the jewelry, but she brushes those possibilities aside like troublesome dust bunnies.

Later that week, I arrive at my mom's house, and I'm met with brief, icy responses instead of her usual warm, humorous energy. I leave, bewildered by this sudden turn in her personality until Mike tells me my aunty suggested to my mom and grandma that since I had broken into Grandma's house and stolen items as a child, I was the suspect for the now missing jewelry.

The next day, I head to my grandmother's. I tearfully explain I would never do anything to hurt her and that my relationship with her is so precious to me. Again, her eyes dart suspiciously back and forth, refusing to look at me. She has lost her trust and perhaps her love for me.

I speed up the street to my parents' home where they are on the porch with a man I don't recognize. With tears staining my cheeks, I choke out rhetorical inquiries, trying to decipher why they believe in someone else's accusations when I have given them no reason to mistrust me. I have lived a good life for many years, being a dutiful daughter, wife and mother, but it seems that the actions of my past dictate their understanding of who I am.

"Val, we're talking with the insurance agent now. This isn't a good time," my mom says as she gestures to their guest on the porch.

"I don't want you to ever see the kids again!" I tell them.

"We can't even visit?" Mom asks.

"I refuse to teach my children it's okay for you to accuse me of something I haven't done!" I cry. "And you didn't even ask me about it!"

"I can come back at another time," says the visitor, trying to leave.

"No! You stay, I'm leaving!" I tell him.

Later, I try to discuss the issue with my father over the phone. He is dismissive after learning I had donated jewelry to a local high school band fundraiser. I tell him I can prove that I gifted items of my own design and creation but my father is set, believing I was now trying to absolve myself of guilt by disposing of stolen evidence.

I slam the phone down, grief gripping my body. I slump to the floor, sobbing. My mother-in-law comes over and hugs me.

"How can your family think that of you?" she asks. "You would never do such a thing."

She holds me while I cry, my heart hollow.

HONEYMOON OVER

Mike's family would joke we were still on our honeymoon every time they saw us hugging or holding hands, even after being married for a number of years. So, one night as Mike returned to bed after a midnight trip to the bathroom, I was saddened to hear him say, "Honeymoon over." I couldn't understand why he would say such a hurtful thing and asked him. He laughed and replied, "I said, 'Honey, *move* over!'"

NO APOLOGIES

My cousin's suggestion slithers out of the phone receiver like a devious snake.

"Admit you did it," he tells me. "Just apologize, and they'll forgive you."

Even if I didn't do it, he rationalizes the family drama will end if I simply admit to stealing Grandma's jewelry. Refusing to listen to his irrational suggestion, I prefer to isolate my children and myself from the family I once relied on so heavily.

Our long-desired dream of moving from O'ahu to Hawai'i Island materializes, and we learn that we can sell our home in two short months. My parents are startled to find their chances of seeing the grandchildren disappearing, with a plane ride separating us, rather than a two-minute drive.

My parents quickly make amends, expediting what healing could occur in the short time during the weeks prior to our departure. After we moved, they called, mailed letters and gifts and visit several times a year. In turn, we did the same, rebuilding and enhancing the relationship as the years passed. My mom later explained that she envisioned her future and knew that the years with her mother and sister were waning, but if she wanted to spend the rest of her life with the kids, she knew that she had to repair her relationship with me.

In September of 2005, my husband, the children and I relocated from my hometown of Wahiawā to the Volcano area of Hawai'i Island. I never returned to visit Grandma and she passed away less than a year after we moved.

III.

MOAI

The elders in Okinawa, Japan, belong to one or more *moai* (pronounced moh-eye), a social support network of people who begin meeting during their childhood. Groups often continue their relationships as they age, some for more than a century since a large number of residents in Okinawa have extended lifespans. Residents often belong to multiple moai, expanding their social and support circles. Originally formed as groups to facilitate social interaction, to pool money for community projects or to help with individual expenses, moai, with the strong social connections they build, contribute to Okinawan longevity.

Similarly, groups like neighborhood *kumiai,* also known as bereavement support, provide assistance to members who have experienced a death in the family. Group members give *koden,* monetary funeral donations to help offset the cost of a funeral service and the reception that follows. During the plantation era in Hawai'i, these small contributions were essential as most families could not afford the cost associated with burial or cremation of a loved one, thus relieving some of the stress associated with the passing of a family member. On Hawai'i Island, I've observed an additional offering of support. Funeral attendees help supplement the post-service reception with desserts and other tasty contributions.

Some families, both from Okinawa and mainland Japan, engage in *tanomoshi,* a yearly pooling of family money, distributed to a different branch of the family during each annual rotation. The receiving members can use the funds to pay off debts, make an investment or pay for an expense that would normally be beyond their means. This allows family members to have more financial stability, especially if a conventional bank would not grant them a loan.

These traditional support groups have different iterations in modern times. Coffee shop meetings, social media groups and crafting clubs provide opportunities for people of different backgrounds and interests to gather and connect.

As I get older, I find that various moai keep my mind, body and spirit engaged and focused on the good in life. There is nothing like feeling loved and valued by those you treasure the most.

ILLUMINATION

I have been a housewife (I prefer the term domestic goddess) and stay-at-home mom (domestic consultant and engineer) since my spouse and I were married in 1997. But in 2003, after our young daughter, Naiʻa, entered preschool and our eleven-month-old son, Nolan, was in his father's capable post-retirement hands, I decided it was time to return to the workforce and the land of adult conversations.

I found a position as assistant store manager and consignment manager in a quaint retail gallery on the North Shore of Oʻahu. At the gallery, I enjoyed interacting with the public, training new employees and overseeing the accounts for over a hundred local artists.

One day, a ceramic artist named J. Forest Ocean Bennett arrived with a number of intriguing ceramic pieces she called "Spiritforms." Embodying various qualities, the sculptures expressed the sacred connection with nature and journey of spirit. I was immediately drawn to her art and her authentic personality. During her visit, she shared that she had somehow hurt her back, and being a licensed massage therapist, I quickly offered her therapeutic bodywork after I was done with work.

We developed a deep friendship. J was my go-to for everything regarding personal and spiritual growth. She was extremely well read, and her travels took her to meet Amma, the Hugging Saint from Kerala, to Black Rock Desert to participate in the Burning Man festival. She also journeyed to South America for an *ayahuasca* retreat.

After moving off-island, I maintained our relationship with letters and phone calls.

One day, I called J. "Hi, J! Whatcha doing?"

She said, "I'm getting rid of all my books."

I was shocked that she was getting rid of her extensive inventory of self-help and philosophy books. "Why?"

"I only need one book, *The Autobiography of a Yogi* by Paramahansa Yogananda." She had mentioned the book before, but there was no way I was going to read anything that started with the word "autobiography." But with her declaration to remove all other reference books from her life, I knew she had found something significant. I needed to find out what it was.

I dove into the book and participated in two yoga philosophy courses to learn the interconnected nature of many of the world's major religions. I began to meditate and learned more about quieting the mind. The process changed how I viewed the world and my understanding of God. My family was grateful for the calming effect meditation provided me.

But life was messy. After a year, my consistent practice turned inconsistent, then eventually ceased. But it's not gone—when I feel scattered and stressed, I sit down, close my eyes and try to quiet my mind. I think back to how J and I met, and how fortunate I am to have found a friend who shared her journey, which helped me grow into a wiser and better person.

LIKE FAMILY

I hear the familiar whir of a weed whacker in the distance and rush to cut pieces of cornbread, fresh out of the oven. It's my mother's recipe, topped with melted butter and sticky honey. I place them on a paper plate and cover it loosely with shiny tinfoil.

I stroll toward the home of our closest neighbors, set more than three hundred feet away from our new house in the rainforest. Two people are outside, steadily cutting back the verdant growth as I step onto their driveway. A middle-aged man with a deep Kona coffee complexion stops his weed whacker to greet me and introduces himself as Larry. His wife, a slightly taller jovial white woman of the same age, introduces herself as Sandy. They gracefully receive the cornbread and thank me.

This encounter opens the door to dog sitting exchanges, chats over each other's gates and family gatherings. Despite COVID-19 putting a damper on socializing, we continue to stay connected. We look forward to any gathering with Larry's amazing pork *adobo* with the secret ingredient. And Larry's face lights up when he sees my daughter's homemade kimchi, especially when it's a quart-size jar or larger, darkly shaded by the deep red chili pepper flakes inside. Our favorite exchange is the time we share together, and I realize that friends can become family too.

THE FAMILIAR STRANGER

I was a new devotee of Paramahansa Yogananda, the yogi who brought yoga to the West, and was excited to attend my first Convocation with the Self-Realization Fellowship in Los Angeles, California. I joined my dear friend J and two new friends at the annual event where I learned to refine my spiritual practice and had the opportunity to travel to sacred pilgrimage sites.

I arrived at the Los Angeles International Airport and boarded a prearranged shuttle that took me to my hotel. Passengers filled the van and with each stop, one or two departed. As we drove through the darkened streets toward the next destination, the young woman seated next to me dramatically lowered her voice an entire octave and informed me that we were entering "the hood." She laughed, and her voice returned to normal.

She asked if I was visiting or returning home. I told her I had traveled to LA for Convocation. She asked me what it was, and I did my best to describe what I knew. I confessed I was a new participant and uncertain as to what to expect. She thanked me as she departed the shuttle in front of her home that looked more like it was in a normal middle-class suburb rather than the hood.

I turned to smile at the remaining passenger seated behind me and asked him the question the woman posed to me. Was he in LA for a visit or to return home? He smiled warmly and said that he was headed to the same place I was. If my Asian complexion could blush in embarrassment, it probably did. My insecurity bubbled out of me, and I exclaimed that I hoped I had told the woman the right thing about the event. My co-passenger reassured me that I shared the most important components and informed me that I would be immersed in a truly special event. The shuttle pulled up to the front of the Biltmore Hotel and my new friend said farewell.

During the week, I was surprised to encounter this same individual repeatedly. After circumnavigating the Lake Shrine meditation gardens in the Pacific Palisades area, we talked story while dining on vegetarian Indian food. We discussed the challenges of life and our understanding of spiritual growth. He seemed strangely familiar, and I learned that aside from our spiritual practice and dedication, we had other common beliefs and values.

Later in the week, we crossed paths in the threshold of a ballroom. I was amused, and my face mirrored his expression of surprise and surrender as if it was totally natural that we should see each other again. He had attended the event many times over the years, had several friends who also attended, but he never saw them. And yet, we had seen each other three times in less than six days despite being two individuals amongst thousands of attendees.

I returned the following year, and as the hotel elevator descended to street level on my first day there, the doors opened, and there he was. We each pressed our own hands together in gratitude and bowed to each other. Though each encounter was brief, his presence reminded me that no matter where I go and no matter how alone I feel, behind the face of every friend and stranger is the face of God.

THE TITA NANIS IN KAPOHO

I gaze at a photo of Brenda, Leolani and me drinking mimosas to celebrate my forty-second birthday. The drinks were made by Brenda, the expert in all things festive. Her joyous nature is reflected in her vacation-style home where the photo was taken, her bubbly personality, her frosty alcoholic beverages and her perfectly suited middle name, Joy. Years ago, we would often gather at her beachfront house in Kapoho, the only home free of spouses and kids, to reconnect, celebrate and nurture our friendship.

We called ourselves the Tita Nanis, a fun name we came up with while in Hawaiian language class at the local community college. It was coined to define the three of us who were older than many of the young kids straight out of high school. Brenda often joked that one day, those young ones would be the managers of our Tita Nani Nursing Home, where on-site staff would be composed solely of handsome young Hawaiian men.

With each year that passed, Brenda observed that the harsh weather and accompanying storm surge advancing toward her beloved home located in the

Kapoho Vacationland area of lower Puna. Though the house itself was well situated atop tall pillars and safe from flooding, the downstairs parking area, where her storage shed sat, was not. During a particularly brutal storm, the shed was washed out onto the road opposite the beach. When Brenda returned home in the aftermath of the storm, she recognized personal items floating in the receding waters and lodged in trees. She surrendered to the inevitability of rising ocean levels and put her home up for sale. Marketed as "a personal residence or investment property," it was snatched up quickly by investors who used it as a vacation rental. We were all a bit sad that our personal vacation site had been sold, but we were relieved that Brenda no longer had to worry about the rising ocean and storm damage.

In 2018, the island of Hawaiʻi was jolted by strong earthquakes. Lava seeped out of the earth, inundating the lower East Rift Zone in Puna. The chasm called Fissure 8 sent fast-moving lava toward Kapoho. Watching the riveting news footage, Brenda realized her former home was in the path of the oncoming flow. Survivor's guilt consumed her as she watched her former neighborhood, including the beachfront home she once loved, engulfed by scalding-hot lava. She was grateful she no longer owned the beachfront home, but sorrow for her friends and former neighbors filled her heart. The loss of the nearby Waiʻōpae Tide Pools was additionally difficult since Brenda had been instrumental in securing a grant to create a visitor education program on-site after it had been recognized as a Marine Life Conservation District in 2003.

I am so grateful for the time we spent nurturing our Tita Nani relationship in Brenda's home in Kapoho, but my memories are mixed with sadness for the people who lost their homes, pets and maybe even a few reclusive lives in the fast-moving flow of 2018.

The Tita Nanis in Kapoho, 2015.

CALLING THE RAIN

Once utilized by the US military for target practice, and further decimated by grazing, the island of Kahoʻolawe requires a constant infusion of native vegetation outplanting. With less than twenty-five inches of rainfall each year, Kahoʻolawe lacks the abundant greenery prevalent on the east side of most Hawaiian islands. Further complicating rehabilitation efforts, Kahoʻolawe sits in the rain shadow of its neighbor, the island of Maui.

In March of 2015, I visited Kahoʻolawe, also known as Kanaloa Moku, with my mom, my two children and several dear friends, including Brenda and Leolani. Many members of our group had knowledge of native Hawaiian plant life and were Hawaiian cultural practitioners of *hula* (traditional dance), *lawaiʻa* (fishing) and other indigenous practices. The goal of our visit was to continue the ongoing replanting efforts in areas that had been cleared of ordnance and deemed safe.

Upon our arrival, we were taken to Puʻu ʻO Moaʻula Nui, to give *hoʻokupu,* offerings of water and a *lei* of *lehua* blossoms made by Brenda. Leolani shared her voice and spirit through *oli*, traditional Hawaiian chant, as the offerings were presented upon the *ko'a*, a shrine dedicated to summoning rain. That night, as we spoke to our hosts about other chants we would share, we heard a familiar sound on the metal roof of the dining hall.

"It's raining!" I exclaimed.

"It never rains here!" said one of the scientists. I swung open the door of the dining hall, and we were greeted by a downpour of rain.

Offerings of water and foliage associated with verdant native plants, along with various chants honoring sacred spaces, manifested our intentions into rain each day we were there.

Nai'a, Nolan, Linda, Leolani, Brenda and Valdeane on the island of Kaho'olawe, 2015.

Linda, Nolan and Nai'a outplanting native species on Kaho'olawe, 2015.

IV.

FACEBOOK GRATITUDE POSTS, 2015–2018

Posted on 11/24/2015, 6:07 a.m. (HST)

In honor of the passing of one of the great teachers in my life last night, I will post what I learned from him during this week of his transition from his body to spirit.

I am grateful for the following lessons from my former band director, Keith Fukumoto:

1. Be open to receiving love.

While visiting Keith in the hospital, I saw how receptive he was to receiving love from those who visited. He was sincere with his gratitude and could hear their messages of concern with no shying away or false appreciation.

2. Enjoy life.

Even at the hospital, while having a challenging time breathing, he ate the ice cream brought by family to celebrate his birthday.

3. Be focused. Time is precious.

   Don't let others waste your time.

   I observed that Keith was very alert. When he felt like time was wasting, he verbally gave cues to move the conversation or activity along so that he could spend time with visitors and/or move away from the superfluous.

4. Be present.

   I saw how in his illness, Keith's transition physically kept him in a hospital bed; however, that created opportunity for sacred space to be held in that room. Ensuring he (and Shari) knew how loved they were was my priority at that moment.

5. It's all about relationships.

   Keith wasn't teaching us about music, he was teaching us about our relationships with the world and each other.

   Show the people you love that they matter. Now.

   Nurture the relationships that nurture you. Release others that don't.

Posted on 1/1/2016, 1:33 p.m. (HST)

On this first day of 2016, I want to first speak (type) words of gratitude for my family and our continued love, health and growth.

Just to let you all know, my husband suffered a minor stroke on Sunday the 27th after we returned from Oʻahu.

The effects were seemingly minor and with therapy, he should get better.

For now, he's listening to his body, not overdoing anything and being patient with himself and this new "normal."

We never take our days for granted, but this event was just another reminder of how we need to treasure each other, love those who nurture us and rid our lives of anything that does not serve our highest good.

Blessings to you all, dear friends and family.

May 2016 bring you joyous growth, love and contentment.

Posted on 7/26/2017, 10:59 p.m. (HST)

I am grateful for all the time I've had this summer to support Mike's change in health after his second stroke, prepping for Nai'a's departure to Northern Arizona University in August and clearing out the house and workshop in order to simplify life due to Mike's diminished strength and capacity.

I am grateful the kids went to O'ahu to enjoy time with my parents.

But I'm also looking forward to getting a teaching job since most of my cohort members have already been hired. If not, I'll have to think about opening a shop or something...well, that has been my longtime dream anyway.

Taking deep breaths and keeping the faith.

Posted on 6/5/2018, 7:43 p.m. (HST)

I finally have time to acknowledge those who helped to support me during my first year of teaching at Nā'ālehu Elementary School.

When my classmate, Rose, asked if I would consider a long-term substitute position in a first grade classroom, I was a bit nervous since I trained for secondary education. But the principal, Darlene Javar, the friendly staff and faculty members put me at ease, with their encouragement and support.

With each day, week and month that passed, I came to enjoy the small rural school and community. And as much as I scolded those kids, I came to love those sweet little souls and the rascal ones too! I hope they left my class knowing a little more about life and how to behave!

Posted on 12/29/2018, 11:03 p.m. (HST)

Okay universe, I'm pau with 2018.

Two tires on the riding mower have been punctured and needed fixing.

Mike collapsed twice and we learned he has mini bleeds in his brain due to a genetic disorder.

HiloDog went to the vet for different ailments as he approached the grand age of sixteen.

So many people passing, too many job changes, and today I slipped while trying to close the gate and scraped a deep hole in my knee.

Think we've satisfied this year's requirements for unpleasantries.

On the upside, my kids and parents are happy and healthy. Mike can still get around and help. I have amazing friends and family who support us. Nai'a and Nolan are getting stronger, more skilled and more loving with each day. Mika doesn't chew things she shouldn't anymore and unlike a few years back, our vehicles are working well!

I am grateful for all the blessings in our lives.

But I'm ready for a gentler year for sure!

BROKEN

Made in China

I hear the dull whack of something hitting the kitchen floor. I wince, knowing it's the special Yixing clay teapot I use specifically for herbs the Chinese medicine practitioner prescribed me. Mike's face is apologetic as I uncontrollably shout at him in anger. Upset and disappointed, I gently caress the remaining cover. A near perfect replica of a lotus blossom, complete with loosely held clay lotus "seeds" that softly rattle within the crevices of the intricate cover.

No Mo' Joe

Crack. I rush toward the sound that emanates from the kitchen and find glass shards at Mike's feet. It's my coffee pot. Upset, I ask, "What happened?" Mike shrugs and says, "It just slipped out of my hands." I instruct him to stay still while the children and I pick up the shards and sweep up the cracked glass, allowing him to move after everything is cleared.

Broken Window, Ass Why Hahd!

Dad had flown in from O'ahu to renovate Nai'a's room, gifting her with the installation of a custom-built window seat and bookshelves. The entire family was tasked with assisting as Dad's apprentices and laborers. His years as a carpenter foreman was evident as he directed us to support him by carrying materials, continuous cleanup and helping with construction and installation of pieces of the project.

We're beginning to relax after a particularly tiring day of helping Dad demolish a section of Nai'a's bedroom when I hear Mike leave the house and head to the workshop. Nolan soon realizes Mike has been gone for a while, so he heads out to the shop to check on his dad. I hear Nolan call out, "Help! Help! Dad needs help!" I rush out the back door and down the steps to the shop to find Mike in a partially seated position on the ground, his legs awkwardly splayed out in a squat as he's struggling to hold up six sheets of plywood that are threatening to crush him. The sight of Mike is frightening and comical at the same time as I notice his backside has broken through one pane of the six-foot sliding window that was set across the walkway.

Nolan helps me lift the plywood sheets and lean them back on the workroom table where they were originally set as my father enters the shop to help. Nolan helps Mike up off the floor. We make sure he isn't injured or has glass stuck on him. I ask, "What happened?" Mike says, "I needed something from the table and thought I could hold the plywood." I scold, "You could have cut yourself, and what if Nolan didn't hear you? What if you got cut, bled out and died!" He says sorry before heading into the house to shower and change his clothes while my father, the children and I clean up the glass.

Broken Cups, WHAT THE FUCK?!

Mike is staying with my parents during his visit with friends and family on O'ahu. My dad decides to take the opportunity to have Mike deliver a special gift to me and calls ahead to excitedly inform me he found more than a dozen Japanese *somayaki* teacups at the local swap meet. The teacups are known for the distinctive crackled green glaze and double walls, and Dad knows he's found a small treasure. He will send them them home with Mike. Since Dad's gifts are few and far between, I'm delighted to receive the unusual cups.

Upon arriving home, Mike plops a large flat-rate USPS box on the table and the sound of multiple ceramic shards are heard within. I open the unsealed cover to find more than half of the cups shattered. The cups have minimal protection between them. I ask Mike, "What happened? Why didn't you wrap them between your clothes to protect them on the flight?" Mike shrugs and replies, "I thought they were wrapped already. I thought they'd be okay." "Didn't you hear them breaking as you handled your bag?!" Tears run down my cheeks as I remove what remains intact, leaving the broken pieces to be discarded with the box.

Bowled Over

As I'm putting away dishes, I hear a *clink* as I place one of my favorite bowls away. I pull it out to find it cracked along the side, the latest victim of Mike's aggressive dish handling. I sigh and toss it in the trash. I try to convince myself that with each favorite item lost, I'm learning to release my attachment to physical things. It's like my very own Buddhist torture. I mean teachings. I chuckle at my Freudian slip. At least I can still joke about it.

STEERING AHEAD

Mike purchased a secondhand *wa'a* from an ad he saw online. The small outrigger canoe was barely big enough for our family of four, but Mike assured me it would fit all of us, and he would use it to teach the children to fish. Mike had received a few sailing lessons from the seller and insisted he was ready to sail.

Mike repainted the wa'a, made additions to the trailer, then announced he was ready to take the family out on the ocean. We decided the inaugural journey would coincide with the day the two double-hull, deep-ocean voyaging canoes, *Hōkūle'a* and *Hikianalia,* departed Hilo Bay for the 2014 Worldwide Voyage.

At first, our time on the wa'a was pleasant. Nai'a and I paddled, with Nolan seated between us. However, after fifteen short minutes out in Hilo Bay, we quickly approached rocks jutting out of the water. With Mike in charge of steering at the rear of the wa'a, Nai'a and I glanced back to ask if we should continue to paddle forward. It was Mike's job as steersman to move us away from the rocks but it soon became apparent that we were still headed toward danger.

Our questions rose to the level of urgent shouting for guidance but Mike gave no response and there was no change in direction. I began to paddle hard on one side of the canoe and luckily Naiʻa intuitively followed to help change our course so we could avoid the rocks and head toward shore.

The children lost faith in Mike's ability to keep them safe on the waʻa. Later, we noticed the waʻa had not been properly upgraded or maintained. A less-than-detailed paint job, inappropriate lashing and other issues reflected Mike's slowly diminishing abilities.

NOTES FOR THE DOCTOR

There has been an overall decrease in Mike's physical strength, balance and mental awareness. He has a harder time recalling names, phone numbers, planning and explaining or providing details. Additional details are listed below.

CHANGES IN SPEECH/LANGUAGE: Mike has difficulty forming sentences and he pauses more frequently when speaking. He uses aggressive language and tone during conversation and task-based interactions.

PHYSICAL CHANGES: We notice an overall weakness in Mike's body, along with less coordination when walking. He often trips and drags his feet. He is unsteady upon rising from seated position, despite repeated instruction to plant feet before standing and walking. He stumbles immediately after standing. He gets tired faster, obvious by the slack look of his eyes and face. His posture is continuing to degrade.

LOGIC: Mike exhibits a general lack of understanding or concern regarding safety, procedure and hygiene.

OTHER: Decreased ability to recognize joking behavior, gets angry quicker than before. Less patient with son. Lack in awareness/sensitivity for others and situations of others.

Mike pushes himself beyond his limits when working without recognizing that he will be overtired later. His work becomes sloppy or unsafe when he is fatigued. He doesn't recognize the correlation between being tired and the ability to work safely. We encourage him to take breaks or stop since he has all the time in the world to complete projects, but he continues to dismiss our recommendations. Suggestions, please.

2018 HOLIDAY NEWSLETTER

Greetings, friends and family! The weather is beginning to cool and the daylight dims earlier in the evenings. I feel the rush of the holiday season approaching and wanted to share a bit about our year before it comes to an end.

Mike had a couple of setbacks this year after overexerting himself doing yard work. The first event occurred in February, while Naiʻa was still in Arizona. Nolan called 911 and a couple of neighbors came over to help. Paramedics checked Mike out and stated he was okay. In the weeks following, Nolan and I noticed that Mike was having trouble with different tasks, so I took Mike for a checkup. We soon learned he has a genetic disorder where he is prone to microbleeds in his brain, essentially, mini strokes. The second event occurred in early September and luckily Nolan caught Mike as he lost balance and collapsed. Naiʻa called 911and notified me via phone since I was on Oʻahu with my parents. Both events were due to a combination of exhaustion, uneven ground, dehydration and Mike's lack of awareness of his energy levels. Fortunately, both kids were able to respond appropriately when needed.

Nolan (age 16) passed the High School Equivalency Test (HiSET) in May and registered for a college class in the fall. In early summer, Nolan was fortunate enough to acquire blacksmithing equipment from the estate of a well-known Volcano resident.

Sadly, in June, Mike's mom was admitted to hospice. He flew back and forth to see her, spending time with her before the family left for a trip to Arizona to help Nai'a move back home from Northern Arizona University. Unfortunately, Mike's mom passed while the family was away, but Mike was glad he spent time with her before he had left the Islands.

Nai'a (age 19) thrived during her time in Flagstaff. She excelled in her classes, enjoyed the seasonal weather and built strong friendships with exceptional individuals who helped her grow as a person. She was an excellent "mother hen" to her roommates and neighbors, where her responsibility and homemaking skills helped keep her new friends alive and well fed. While in Arizona, Nai'a visited the Grand Canyon, Antelope Canyon, Horseshoe Bend, the Petrified Forest and other sites. Our entire family enjoyed meeting Nai'a's fun roommates and quirky neighbors. Nai'a is pushing hard to graduate at the end of 2019 with degrees in art and geography.

During the Arizona trip, Nolan got to meet Vince Evans, a skilled blade maker from Hawai'i who now resides in Arizona with his wife, Grace. Vince shared various tips and tricks that helped Nolan refine his knife making. Since returning home, Nolan has worked steadily to improve his skills in blade making and other crafts.

Nolan is doing exceptionally well in his college class, though he often wants to (respectfully) highlight the instructor's oversight of certain elements of history. Nolan continues to work hard, along with Naiʻa, both caring for the property.

In September, after Mike's second collapse, I decided to resign from my teaching position to stay home and better support Mike and the kids. I've been using my time to heavily purge the excess clutter from the house and get Mike out more often.

Grandpa and Grandma spent Thanksgiving with us and the kids are looking forward to seeing them on Oʻahu for winter break. I will close here and wish you all the best as the year comes to a close. Don't forget to make time for those who matter to you. You'll never regret the memories you made together!

EVERYTHING IS NOT OKAY

Dirty dishes in the dish rack. Oily surfaces, bits of stuck food, some dishes appear to not have been washed at all. I center myself and place the dirty dishes back in the sink. Some need to soak while I attend to the easier grime.

Mike enters the kitchen. Do I repeat the instructions of washing dishes, or do I ignore it? I can't help myself, so I remind him. *Wash the dishes with the lights on. Look at the dish while you're washing, don't just stare off into space mindlessly. Use the abrasive side of the washing sponge. Use hot water. Feel for oil and stuck-on food. Rinse well.*

He stares blankly, then says, "Okay." He continues to move about the kitchen. I take another breath, swallowing my sorrow and frustration, and return to rewashing the dishes.

I remind him that he's welcome to wash his own dish, but to not wash the cooking dishes or anything with a lot of oil or heavy staining.

"Okay," he says again.

I remind him that we appreciate him putting away the dishes but when he washes, we often need to rewash them.

"Okay," he repeats flatly.

"Okay," I reply.

LIGHTEN THE LOAD

It seemed easy to eliminate things I once felt were precious. Out went hats and bags I wove out of *lauhala,* the pliable yet study leaves of the pandanus plant. Craft supplies meant to be turned into meaningful gifts and books waiting to be read were removed from my home. I released gifts given by others, items I purchased or shells and beach glass gathered from the shores of the ocean. Some treasures found new homes with friends, and some were sold during a yard sale. Much was donated and some were trashed.

At first, the purge was in response to Mike's most recent stroke. I knew I wouldn't have time for personal pursuits after his physical strength and cognitive ability decreased. I was grateful my daughter led the first round of elimination in the house and shop, motivated by the fact she was leaving for a year of student exchange in Arizona. She wrangled her brother into helping her consolidate their father's fish collection and helped me organize and prep for the yard sale. She left for school knowing she did her best to reduce the amount of work her brother and I would need to do.

As I continued to purge items I once deemed special and removed them from the home, I began to feel as if I was purging myself out of the house in the process. I felt resentful, believing that my life was no longer my own, and I needed to simplify to keep up with Mike's changing health. I kept my earbuds in, listening to music and audiobooks to avoid interacting with others, fearful my emotions would overflow into the newly available spaces, made empty by my purging.

WEED WHACKING WILLPOWER

Living in rural East Hawai'i, without access to county water, rain is our water source. Captured in the corrugated grooves of our *totan* (corrugated metal) roof, rainwater runs through three-inch PVC pipes to a large, circular metal tank behind our home. Within the tank, a food-grade liner holds our water before it is summoned to the home via a large pump, passing first through a three-stage filtration system and UV light for additional sterilization. The tank is scheduled to be cleaned today and it's up to me to clear the dense grass, weeds and moss surrounding the tank before the cleaner arrives later that morning.

Our two weed whackers have been acting up, so I pray at least one starts easily. The first is lighter and easier to manage so I try it first. I click the switch on, prime the line with fuel by pumping the grimy rubber nob on the side of the engine, ensure the choke is on, then pull the cord. Once, twice, three times. Once more. The little engine gives quiet little rumbles with each pull, but it doesn't turn over. I try again. I check the tank; there is adequate fuel, so I try a few more times. Pull, pull, pull, pull, rest. Try again. Pull, pull, pull, pull, stop. I look at the other, larger weed whacker and decide to try that one instead. It, too, refuses to start. I try multiple times and finally ask my daughter to help. We eventually call her brother who is off-island, visiting my parents on Oʻahu. He walks us through, and the large weed whacker finally roars to life.

I wear a backwards hat to protect my hair, a face shield, safety glasses and earplugs. I tighten the strap draped over my shoulder and secure the machine to my side as I promptly get to work clearing a large path from the covered lānai toward the catchment tank. The intertwined moss and grass are abundantly dense. Moving side to side in a sweeping motion doesn't work well so I start using the machine like a helicopter, lifting it over the grass then pushing it down quickly to cut through the mass. I'm quickly exhausted, and it doesn't help that my hat refuses to sit properly on my head along with the face shield and my safety glasses. The hat slips off my head as I reposition the shield. "Fuck it!" I leave the bright aqua hat where it falls as I continue to fight against the greenery.

I recall all the times I took a glass of water or a snack to Mike as he worked outside in the yard. Over the years, I taught our children to do the same. It gave us a chance to make sure Mike was okay, and the refreshments were a sign of appreciation and recognition, the least we could do for someone working so hard. It dawns on me that Mike rarely did the same for me whenever I did the yard, and now after his strokes, he may not be able to consider bringing me a glass of water. Can't or won't? I struggle trying to remember he probably can't, though my heart believes that he doesn't want to. I'm shocked at the loneliness that floods my heart. Without warning, I start to sob uncontrollably but keep working.

My grief turns to anger. I channel the energy to forcefully sweep the weed whacker back and forth, making my way around the tank. I catch a glimpse of my big gray dog darting away from me, the bright aqua blue hat in his mouth. A tear-soaked smile spreads across my lips, and I chuckle in gratitude. "Thanks for grabbing that for me!" I shout in his direction. I take a deep breath, feeling less isolated and grateful for his help. I look around and I notice the work is done.

HONOHONO GRASS

Numerous smothering limbs twist snakelike through the grass, strangling the volunteer tomato vines, forcing them to reach for an empty clearing before suffocating beneath the succulent creeping vine known as *honohono* grass. As I attempt to remove the growing horde near the chicken coop, the long, segmented tendrils tipped with opposing spear tip shaped leaves glimmer in the daylight, hinting at the oncoming battle.

Half cursing myself for neglecting the task and half praising my effort to make it outside to do yard work, I approach the area armed with boots, gloves and a grimace of sheer determination. This is my fourth attempt to clear an area where tomato plants and one precious *shiso* (beefsteak plant) have emerged in the nutrient rich soil around the chicken coop. Although I don't love tomatoes, I feel like a traitor to my farming ancestors if they get choked out by the weeds or I allow them to rot.

The kids wanted to mow the honohono under, but I remind them of my mother's warning of the plant's near impervious nature. I affirm that I will make the effort to eradicate the hydra-like weeds that will simply continue to grow from cut segments. I need to pick up each piece, leaving nothing behind, or it will self-root and regrow.

Yanking at the tangled vines, I realize I'm going against what I expected in life. I'm no longer just a wife who tends to the house while my spouse cares for the yard. I'm no longer a victim of my husband's unfortunate health situation. I'm no longer waiting for things to change. Life is too short to wish for what could have, should have, would have been. I need to move forward and get shit done.

CAREGIVING DOS AND DON'TS:

A.K.A. How to Keep My Sh*t Together

A list of helpful tips to keep me from losing my sh*t and not make more physical or emotional work for myself.

1. Pause. When something upsetting happens, don't react immediately. No eye rolls, sighs of exasperation, swearing, throwing things or storming out of the room, etc. Try to maintain a neutral face.

2. Breathe. Take a deep breath. This will also help with #1 since the breath will stop all other things from happening. Close my eyes if needed. This also helps since I am prone to eyeball rolling.

3. Think. Don't say the first thing that wants to come out of my mouth because it will probably be hurtful.

4. Clasp hands together. Do this to avoid flinging dishes at the wall when I find them in the cabinet

still wet or dirty. Yes, it would be nice to have all the dishes clean and put away properly, but don't act out of anger because then I'll have to clean it up.

5. When tasks go undone or remain incomplete, don't lose my sh*t. Just provide repeat instructions. If that's too frustrating, do steps #1–2 and complete the task myself.

6. Hang in there. It's okay. You can do this.

V.

YEAR OF THE METAL OX

According to Chinese astrology, I was born in the Year of the Ox. The ox is known for being stubborn, dedicated and unyielding. These qualities can manifest in positive ways, but they can also create hardships for those born in the Year of the Ox.

For many years, I have been stubborn, blaming myself for things that were out of my control, or blaming my husband for not nurturing our relationship in the way I wanted. I was dedicated to the belief that I was too fat, too young and lacking in intellect or education. I was unyielding in my belief that I did not provide the ideal level of care for my spouse as he ages and his health wanes.

Clarity came after sessions with my therapist. She helped me understand that caring for someone is difficult and any previous challenges in the relationship will amplify the sorrow and grief I experience. Choosing to remain in a relationship and provide care for a family member is a reflection of who I am, not who they are.

Each twelve-year anniversary of my zodiac heralded change in my life. At age twelve, I took my first trip to the mainland. Four days after my twenty-fourth birthday, I got married. At age thirty-six, I returned to college. 2021, the year of my forty-eighth birthday and the Year of the Metal Ox, has taught me that it's okay to be stubborn, dedicated and unyielding. As long as it helps feed my own growth and self-care.

GLASSES

Straining, peeking, slant-eyed staring
Print too big, screen too close
Back up, back up
Arm too short
Where's my glasses?
Ah…now I see

WRINKLED SKIN

While driving home recently, I glanced down toward the steering wheel and noticed the wrinkled surface of my hands, tanned from recent work on our three-acre property. Both hands are scarred from a lifetime of careless use and too many failed sessions of playing mercy in intermediate school with Kim Nakamura. She quickly twisted my wrists, turning my palms face up as her talon-like nails dug into the backs of my hands. I always admired her long, sharp nails since my own were often chewed down to nubs. Even now, during times of extreme worry and anxiety, my thumbs are often picked red, like raw beef.

Growing up, I had the strongest feeling I would die young. Maybe the multiple visits to the principal's office convinced me I was destined for a life of crime, or maybe it was because I was a daredevil teen who reveled in racing cars on the H-1 freeway, bungee jumping and skydiving.

I arrived home after my drive and stared into the magnifying mirror. The lines on my face reflected the skin on my weathered hands, and I became emotional when I realized that I had lived long enough to see such a physical transformation. Not everyone lives long enough to receive such a gift.

GUIDANCE OF THE ʻIO

On Hawaiʻi Island, there is an endemic and endangered hawk known as the *ʻio*. They are found in various areas and throughout different elevations. They have two color phases, a pale cream and a darker brown. Smaller in size than hawks found elsewhere, they are a welcome sight in the skies above our property.

When we moved to the island of Hawaiʻi in 2005, I took delight in pointing out these lofty visitors to the children. After a while, we noticed they were often seen circling directly above us while we drove or while at home. We assumed it was because the road produced roadkill or their prey was more obvious due to the cleared area.

Sometimes while I was deep in thought, an ʻio would swoop down suddenly, right in front of me. I wondered if they were messengers, meant to capture my attention in that specific moment as I pondered a difficult choice or situation.

Once, when I drove to town, I was thinking about a situation I was debating. A dark-colored ʻio dove from the sky directly in front of my car, abruptly slowing its flight with sharp talons outstretched to capture its prey. In my mind, the message seemed clear—I should take swift and decisive action regarding the issue I had been contemplating.

As I drove home this afternoon, I was feeling very down about my relationship with Mike. Then I noticed an ʻio soaring high above, causing me to look up. My heart suddenly felt a bit lighter and I was reminded that things are not as hard as they seem. Maybe it was coincidence and not guidance, but I know that the message and the messenger are what I believe them to be.

KARMIC RUM CAKE

Newton's third law of motion states that for every action there is an equal and opposite reaction. Like Newton's cradle, the toy with swinging silver orbs that demonstrate motion, I believe that my negative actions will come hurtling back at me like a karmic wrecking ball.

I know I should do all I can to care for my spouse, even if he doesn't want me to. Even if he ignores my reminders or gets irritable. But in order to increase relational harmony, I reduce the constant reminders for him to engage in self-care. Nolan and I monitor his medication and fluid intake, but we no longer push as hard as we used to. Though it helps everyone feel less stressed, this frightens me because I'm worried that when I need care, karma will kick in, and someone will stop caring for me.

I have forgotten that the positive energy I put out in the world returns to me, often from an unexpected source. This was validated when an acquaintance dropped off a package from a mutual friend and, along with it, my favorite rum cake from the Kōloa Rum Company. The wife of the acquaintance had remembered I enjoyed the cake and they carried the two-pound treat on their flight, just for me.

This woman, who is not a relative, close friend or my significant other, remembered this little fact mentioned in passing more than two years ago. The thoughtfulness of the gesture reminded me to stop focusing on bad karma and remember that the good I share with others continues to be gifted back to me, a hundredfold.

WISHES AND RHYMES

When I'm an old woman I will live near the sea
in a cottage surrounded by banana and *ti.*
In a lovely home made of glass and wood,
life will be easy; life will be good.
All day I will play in the sea and the sun,
with salt in my hair and sand on my bum.

When I'm an old woman, I will dance and sing.
I will make all manner of art, craft and thing.
I may not be known for my style and my grace,
but everyone will know me from the smile on my face.
The years have been kind and full of love.
This life that I live fits me like a glove.

My children are grown and I am their friend,
much different when they were aged seven and ten.
The years have enriched the sweet love we share,
and our laughter and jokes are better than fair.
I live a magical life full of friendship and joy,
with my fabulous girl and my wonderful boy.

GENERATIONAL LEGACY

My great-grandmother, Masa Shomi Miyahira—her maiden name pronounced "Soo-mee" in the Ryukyu (Okinawan) language—was a pillar of strength. My grandmother recounted how she and her father would go to the movies and her father would meet a woman there. When Grandma and her father would return home, they would find the door to the house locked, my great-grandmother's protest of her husband's midday matinee rendezvous. In later years, my great-grandmother returned to Okinawa without her spouse to serve her community. She resumed her role as priestess, an intermediary with the spirit world, and provided council to the living.

Grandma Fumiko Miyahira Shiroma's eulogy consisted of the word "kind" repeatedly mentioned and echoed by visitors who filed through the family greeting line to provide words of support. I interpreted her kindness as *gaman,* meaning to hold one's tongue and resist the urge to speak out. She was skilled at it, especially since she married a very grouchy and outspoken man who dominated most conversations.

My mother, Linda Kinuyo Shiroma Uchima, reinforced humility throughout my lifetime. She would become easily irritated or amused by those she found to be arrogant. They were either a nuisance or a character for merriment but overall, arrogance is a trait that she continues to find unacceptable.

I suspect legacy cannot be manufactured or manipulated. It's the actions, interpreted by those impacted that creates someone's legacy. Legacy is the gift we bequeath to those who come after us. What legacy will I leave behind?

MANIFESTO

I live a wholehearted and joyous life.

I don't need to be an artist to create art. I don't need to be a teacher to teach. I don't need to be a dancer to dance. I don't need a label to define who I am. I will simply do what makes me happy!

I no longer waste time regretting the past. Instead, I look at the positive outcomes that occur and new opportunities that open up to me.

I no longer look outside myself for fulfillment, validation or appreciation.

I warmly embrace this body, mind and spirit that I am gifted with.

I have everything I need. I *am* everything I need. I am whole.

NOTE FROM THE AUTHOR

I am in awe of those who learn to voyage across the ocean via traditional methods of navigation, relying on celestial, elemental and animal encounters to guide them. This practice, once the norm in ancient times and in remote locations, has been reestablished over the past forty-plus years in Hawaiʻi. To the unknowledgeable, it may seem like magic or luck, but in truth, it takes training, strong powers of observation, a connection to ancestral knowledge and/or a belief in whatever higher power one holds sacred.

In my youth, I often felt that I was floating along slowly and aimlessly, at the mercy of the currents that surrounded me. During the earlier years of marriage and parental life, I could feel a steady flow, pulling me along the river of easy learning and personal growth. As my spouse's health changed, it seemed I was caught in a maelstrom that would subside, then return with renewed fury with each new health event.

In writing this book and recalling the memories of my life, it helped me see that I was never truly adrift. The challenges of youth allowed me to grow, and through odd synchronicities, the Universe reminds me that I am supported. Despite my uncertainty as I've gotten older, I've found that personal transformation occurs in the ups and downs of life, during the turmoil of relationships and in the moments of supportive friendship.

I hope my book will help readers reflect on their own lives, find gratitude where there was once bitterness or regret and help them recognize the moments of grace that guided them toward change and personal growth.

ACKNOWLEDGMENTS

This book is dedicated to my favorite (only) daughter, Nai'a, and favorite (only) son, Nolan. May you continue to learn and grow into all that you are meant to be. And no matter where your path takes you, I will always be grateful (and proud, yes PROUD) to be your mama.

Oh, and remember to drink enough water and eat your veggies too!

Mahalo to the Hali'a Aloha team, specifically Darien for the effervescent energy that pushed me through. Much gratitude to our spring 2021 cohort of dedicated storytellers, especially Adrienne who helped motivate me and remind me I'm not alone in the writing process.

Deep love to George and Norma Nakasone, who continue to remind me that I am seen, heard and valued.

A fond mahalo to Mike, my parents, family, and friends for all they do to support me on my journey.

Mahalo to my Tita Nanis for all the aloha and festive beverages we share. To J, for the spiritual path you pave for me, I am ever grateful to follow…though sometimes unsteadily. Mahalo to those who take the time to nurture our friendship over the years—Gail, Shari, Sarah and many others. Many thanks to my supervisor/boss-babe Shayna who let me take time off to get my writing done. Ayrica, thanks for being part of our household and helping out! Couldn't have gotten this done without you, Nai'a and Nolan picking up the slack as I wrote, revised and procrastinated!

Valdeane Uchima Odachi is a postsecondary academic counselor and educator who hated school as a child, but now holds various credentials ranging from a Hawaiʻi state license in massage therapy to a master of arts in teaching from the University of Hawaiʻi at Hilo. *Navigating Change* is her first book.

Valdeane was raised in Wahiawā, Oʻahu, by parents Linda and George Uchima but has lived on Hawaiʻi Island since 2005. She is married to Mike, a retired public school elementary educator, and is a mother to two young adults. Her daughter Naiʻa is a multifaceted artist/geospatial analyst/home renovator/kimchi maker/organizer extraoidinaire. Her son Nolan is a kooky and knowledgeable bladesmith/fabricator/history buff of most things sharp and pointy.

Valdeane enjoys teaching the art of Zentangle®, organizing and removing clutter from her home, spending time with family and helping her kids develop their small businesses with shameless plugs. Please check them out on Instagram @sweetbeenotes @odachiforge.